THE REGRET HISTORIES

The National Poetry Series was established in 1978 to ensure the publication of five poetry books annually through five participating publishers. Publication is funded annually by the Lannan Foundation, Amazon Literary Partnership, Barnes & Noble, The Poetry Foundation, The PG Family Foundation and The Betsy Community Fund, Joan Bingham, Mariana Cook, Stephen Graham, Juliet Lea Hillman Simonds, William Kistler, Jeffrey Ravetch, Laura Baudo Sillerman, and Margaret Thornton. For a complete listing of generous contributors to The National Poetry Series, please visit www.nationalpoetryseries.org.

2014 COMPETITION WINNERS

Monograph
by Simeon Berry of Somerville, MA
Chosen by Denise Duhamel for University of Georgia Press

The Regret Histories
by Joshua Poteat of Richmond, VA
Chosen by Campbell McGrath for HarperCollins

Let's Let That Are Not Yet : Inferno
by Ed Pavlic of Athens, GA
Chosen by John Keene for Fence Books

Double Jinx
by Nancy Reddy of Madison, WI
Chosen by Alex Lemon for Milkweed Editions

Viability
by Sarah Vap of Venice, CA
Chosen by Mary Jo Bang for Penguin Books

ALSO BY JOSHUA POTEAT

Ornithologies

Illustrating the Machine That Makes the World

THE REGRET HISTORIES

·

POEMS

·

JOSHUA POTEAT

HARPER  PERENNIAL

NEW YORK • LONDON • TORONTO • SYDNEY • NEW DELHI • AUCKLAND

HARPER ● PERENNIAL

HarperCollins books may be purchased for educational, business, or sales promotional use. For information, please e-mail the Special Markets Department at SPsales@harpercollins.com.

Poems have been previously published, sometimes in different form, in: *Blackbird:* "Drug Department," "Lighting Department," "Memorial Department," "Department of (Aerial) Photography"; *Broad Street:* "Department of Names (*Curiosities of Puritan Nomenclature*)"; *Diode:* "Department of Taxidermy," "Department of Purchase & Disease"; *Gulf Coast:* "Veterinary Department," "Department of Telescopes"; *Greatcoat:* "Department of Hymnals"; *Pilot Light: A Journal of 21ˢᵗ Poetics and Criticism:* "Letter to Gabriel Written in the Margins of Murder Ballads"; *The Southern Review:* "Department of Acoustic Appliances," "Death of the Death of Youth."

For the Animal was published as a chapbook from Diagram/New Michigan Press, 2013.

"Memorial Department" was part of a light-based installation created in collaboration with Roberto Ventura for InLight 2009, which won Best in Show.

FIRST EDITION

Title page and part title pages artwork © jumpe/Shutterstock, Inc.

Designed by William Ruoto

Library of Congress Cataloging-in-Publication Data

Poteat, Joshua, 1971–
  [Poems. Selections]
  The regret histories / Joshua Poteat. — First edition.
     pages ; cm
  ISBN 978-0-06-241223-2
  I. Title.
  PS3616.O843A6 2015
  811'.6—dc23
                    2015016832

15 16 17 18 19 OV/RRD 10 9 8 7 6 5 4 3 2 1

For Jake Adam York

CONTENTS

TWO

THREE

FOUR

I meant to write about death, only life
came breaking in as usual.

—VIRGINIA WOOLF

———————

The dead, the dead, the dead—*our* dead . . .
all, all, all, finally dear to me.

—WALT WHITMAN

TINTYPE

Whole forests went to sea

            disguised as ships.

        Whole seas went to forest

disguised as time.

ONE

DRUG DEPARTMENT

I'm looking for a story that will light
my way out, a star in the sycamore's grass,
taken from night and nothing and limbs cut
back from the wires. It is not summer,
there is no mist on the streets.
The yard, vacant with ivy and nest, wears brown,
and the streetlights. The sycamore is the loudest tree,
its bark lifting the hard wind like the saint
who prayed to the east and failed, parchment
spread on the monastery roof. *Help me*
spelled out in supplicant ink, roaring through
clots of frost. Look at us, late winter, pulling dead
branches from the fence at night to avoid the neighbors,
poison pushed under the shed for the rats.
Let's surrender all illusions of spirit, because it deceives us.
The spirit is not air, even in its highest form,
no matter who sparks the flame.
Tonight, I suffer from not knowing
how to suffer. Tomorrow will be the same.
There used to be pills to cure this affliction.
Early decay, feebleness of will, *Wonderful Little Liver Pills.*
Beef, Iron and Wine for the poorest blood, for fever
of the known and unknown world.
The sycamore leans its branches on the telephone lines.
To hear them on the phone, those manuscripts of bark
breathing the wires, does nothing for my courage.
This is how you become a saint: translate the ruins,

wherever they sleep. Bloom the tulip tree early
and watch bees gather in the sleet. There is no abyss,
no oblivioned ocean. Just a landscape, like this one,
born from a river and seven hills, bones under
the hospital cobbles, ghost rope taut in the gallows.
The glad bees orphan their hive, too soon and unwise.
It isn't death I want, but it isn't life, either.

DEPARTMENT OF PURCHASE & DISEASE

Ghost in the yard, early morning,
the hammock swinging on its own. Rather,
I saw myself reflected in the window
and wanted it to be a ghost, early morning,
the hammock filled with wrens.
Any sign would be enough.
The childhood fear returns, you're thinking,
nostalgia buried within, held to the shallows,
but it's more complicated.
This is 1900.
There are many things to purchase.
There's more than just dying here.
Disease is a good enough excuse,
but this isn't disease.
We just don't know we're changing,
or what we're changing into.

TINTYPE

Between the new ruin

        and the old,

     clover spreads like milk

through the folds.

LIGHTING DEPARTMENT

Soon into the night with him.
—BORIS PASTERNAK

There are bulbs made now to match the light of 1900,
7-watt filament barely a flame, soft as a fever's ear,
where sepia is made, where milk is drawn by cloth
and whale, and moths turn their brief heads from the
    woolens.
Dark was different then—pure, indivisible, a nothingness
moving toward us out of the stars. Afternoon came
unbroken, July in the trees, tallow and beeswax, nothing
the dark couldn't handle. Twilight is what hurt the most,
when the soul pulled the body to the low sky
and every good thing looked inward, belonging
not to itself, but to another older province,
early owl, open field, children in the foliage,
briar and rust. It was a time when lamp blisters
were healed with a round of butter or boiled jewelweed
rended from sewer banks. *Little puck lamp burning*
lavender and clove, 90 cents. Library lamp
bright as 75 candles, $6.50.
The century lends its light to the evening
so that it might have substance, or sight.
The little white throats of pigeons lined up
in the eaves, the new gaslights on 25th Street
imitating the old gaslights, our faces young
in the warmth, something I might already believe.

It's amazing sometimes to find I'm still not dead
here. The gunshots have become almost friendly,
talkative neighbors building a new tongue,
and the shotgun shells dropped outside the market
roll unspent and certain in the wind. I moved into my life
to take it apart, stars dismissed like years
and two fireflies above the crepe myrtle.
Where my house was built a grave was found,
grave of another house, and under that, another grave.
Louis Kahn asked, *What do you want, brick?*
Less grave, more house. Houses live and die,
and to speak of light is a human thing, all the while
the air changes it, creates and re-creates, moves across
the river, cinders of moonlight corroding
the abandoned house down the alley.
From my backyard I can see a sapling growing
on its tin roof, and I know I'm supposed
to look past this, to recognize the syringes and pipes,
condoms and plaster, plate of chicken bones
on a mattress in the gutted kitchen, as a living ruin,
monument to a plague gone courteous at dusk,
but I've seen mud wasps circling the old parlor chandelier,
wary, as if a flame would appear. They knew something
I didn't, so I sat on the mattress to feel the body
of the last century beside me, and there was something
familiar, something lonesome and tired in the design
of mold on the half-eaten walls, wallpaper faded
to powder, and graffiti like veins on the ceiling
spelling out exactly what history has always said:

fuck all y'all this my house. We just weren't listening.
We invent what we need and what we needed
was to see, one frog slurring the night grass,
one sycamore sifting color from the spotted hearts.
This is still the same night, though, the same dew
settled on the bricks, same sorrow, same signal
from them to us: keep the story straight.
The centuries will float to me . . . out of the darkness,
light flooding a mattress, maybe there were wings.
Take my word for it, bats falling through
the street's unlit rooms, ghost bird, ghost hand,
pale ghost of mouse and bulb brought from the hollow oak
that is now only a stump with a sidewalk built around it.
That much I can give of those days.
Because we were infinite then, the night bore us up,
all the burdens of men and animals, headless, dun-kept,
swinging their lanterns against the other world.

DEPARTMENT OF HYMNALS

The night has used itself up, the river, unbound, turns away
and the highway turns to disquiet, trucks downshifting
the overpass, engine upon engine of early morning,
sweet diesel thick as wool and all that peaceful asphalt
sympathetic through the horizon. Not exactly peaceful,
just *there,* a vessel uniform and open, free from
any other purpose, curled by the office buildings,
yellow windows still lit with no memory, no guilt.
There is someone up there throughout the rain,
holding up the sky. Here the years, here the wind,
here the spotlight on the strip club's roof
circling the clouds. *The year before I die*
I shall send out four hymns to track down God.
There will be no answer. Am I wrong to mention God?
No one can tell the living from the shovels of the dead,
which is an example of faith, which is morning.
The highway does not subtract, it adds something,
luminous text of reflective paint makes the city whole,
a new dead voice, bridges stained green to match the eels
in the mud, the girders do not know whether to flourish
or rust, a form of groveling. Passenger, this will hurt a little.
There will be ruin, sedative of fog on the bottomlands
where the plow horses desired not to be touched
in their centuried beds. Before the highway,
there were houses and the deaths of houses,
goldenrod in the slave cemetery, all plowed
under with the city watching. Before that,

something else, trespass and mandate,
osprey at the throat, I listen for it.
The decoy owl on the Masonic Lodge roof
does not scare the pigeons away, so I listen for it.
The pigeons, having never seen a fake owl, listen close
for any sound, sleeping or violence like the bluest eye
of seed rising up. This is why they are born.
Don't hold it against me. To damage takes lessons
in vanishing, and here I am, steeled against death,
no sleep in days, I'm not going anywhere.
There is nothing I won't do to live this life.
One day I'll need to know why.

TINTYPE

Like any good silence,

        night was built

    in the belly

of the hollow field.

DEPARTMENT OF TELESCOPES

It seemed like suffering, or a lesser form of anguish,
though I'm not sure where it comes from,
watching the possum choose an eggshell
from the garbage can, there in the black orchard
of this minor city, the streetlight's hum so peculiar,
clumsy nest bright above the alley. I knew right then
the earth loved it more than me. A city possum,
no *o*, no rat, two babies asleep on its back
and a hunger shot through with fear, with purpose.
In the awkwardness of its living, I feared the city
would abandon me. The possum, too.
I had grown accustomed to its visits.
It lived under the abandoned house down the street,
where the prostitute's body was found last winter,
where the walls grow gentle with rot, a gentleness
gone wrong, harm and permanence, whole and flaw.
Everything is sacrificed to something. To fill the spaces,
I guess. Ash in the trees, then the two stars come out,
the only ones the city allows, little-blue-star-pale-in-its-cups,
little-junkie-track-marks-thanks-for-nothing.
The city has two mouths, the river and the sky,
both brown in the darkness, and open.
More than likely, there is a place inside the body
that is not afraid, but I haven't found it yet,
there is no returning. The hills bear down.
The possum is not jealous, moves slow
through the walls. We can lie down in our emptiness.

TINTYPE

The window units anchor

        the day, herons nest the rebar,

    the small sorrows of hills

chalked solid for miles

        with an unfortunate light.

VETERINARY DEPARTMENT

I am trying to bribe you with uncertainty, with danger, with defeat.

—JORGE LUIS BORGES

The way the morning reduces the river, shelves it,
discontinues, will not be able to help us.
I don't know if this is accurate, but it feels accurate,
and sometimes feeling this is enough.
Choose to believe in a thing, and that thing
will accept itself. Will open its doors.
Will hand over the rudder.
The dead do not want us to fail.
I tend to agree with this. After the long storm,
the river rises with the dawn, and the city fills,
floodwall gates wide, coal trains trawling
their old anguish to the power plants, over trestles
like piers tied calm on the quay. It must be beautiful
from the trestle, a river built low and estranged
through a city. The shining abundance.
The wealth of the waters.
And under the hill, the collapsed tunnel's walls
gone tender in the morning, breached hollow,
rupture and cleft: an engine, her men, and the horse
that tried to save them buried one hundred years,
risen in the light, in the broken king's choir of air.
Once I asked a woman, *what do you like better:*
the train or the train's shadow? Now it's either

the bones kept under the hill or *the bone's withered gears,*
marrow wet as honey in this odd dawn. I can't choose.
There is another journey beginning, unexpected,
bones loosen, the flood patient and able. Man and horse
washed clean together, a modern beast of ivory,
what shall we be? Let go, let go, saddleless boat,
nocturne with no door, no suburb of doves, and drift
east past Four-Mile Creek to the bay, mud and catfish
signaling the shallows, sewage and kerosene swirling
to the Navy shipyard where landscape is irrelevant,
but it's ours, too, that illegible tract of rust no gull
can resist, no marsh can trust.
The house going up across the street is doomed.
Not to water, but to an architecture already failed,
though the open beams meet the air with a quiet sort
of affection, bales of insulation pink in the rain
and enough plywood to build a good boat and a box
for the skulls. Last week, pigeons in the fresh foundation
dirt left disappointed, no worm, no crumb, only buckshot
and brick splinters, an old bottle of wire-cut remedy,
made for the bloody flanks of packhorses, long dead.
I've been trying to find a map of the city, when horses
drew the servant trolleys past my house that used to be
a barbed-wire corral, when the living and the dead wore
the same threadbare expression of gaslight and labor.
White all around us, white in the sky. White lily-belly
of a storm off to marry its one bright love.
The dead do not know who I am. I am lucky in this way.
Tonight will be the same dark as the last, no electricity

for days, the trains on the trestle calling to the train
buried under the hill, to the bloated century in the river.
I can see why some think ghosts are imprints left over
from the habit of living. Even a buried train has a ghost.
It is a horse. It is kicking through the hill and the years
and the bones of years where the hidden world
holds the other close. I am sure of it.
Nothing else will remedy our awe.
No other night will find the flood
and make us whole again.

DEATH OF THE DEATH OF YOUTH

I see the summer children in their mothers,
in the way the womb chose them
to live, fingers veined
into the alley oaks, night bursts
their throats, no signal moon.
The power out again, I listen
for a whistle or car horn,
something I might know
in all that dark.
Now the kids are in the street
graphing new homes with their voices,
a living sound, a wound of air
I do not understand.
Their hands knead the asphalt,
one throws half a brick and the blood
that arrives unseen is no one's.
The noise of time is not sad,
it's diagrammed somewhere inside
the land. We honor this emptiness.
A door appears, a flame.
A girl at the end of the block lights
a cigarette, her face assembled from
radiance and the acres.
The loneliness of her, of me watching
her, the nothingness of me, of this room,
the receding storm pinioned to the sky.
In 1900, an accountant built this house

to carve his name on an attic beam—
laudanum-sweat through the plaster.
The regret of his name there,
as if it could conceive, then hurt.
The regret history assembles
by the highway, the projects,
the cemetery, all stacked up,
dissected, is not hungry.
Walter forecloses next door
and mold rises through the sheriff's
arms, clothes spread on the sidewalk
for the rats to tame and sweeten.
Everyone has a flashlight, a gun.
Who kills my history? the kids should yell,
spoons carving the sides of cars.
I am the man your father was, I think.
We are the sons of flint and pitch.
I do not exist for us.
The past has failed into shapes
as if light gathered form
from the air, and gave to it a body—
the weeds bowing in every direction,
in mercy and indifference.

TINTYPE

Early morning,
                minor starlight.

      In the oak leaves,

the heat's pulse.

      In the alley,

crickets and old hives,

         sailor-suited, among

the brick and bottle shards.

      My shards, *my* oak,

         a whole new astronomy.

DEPARTMENT OF NAMES (*CURIOSITIES OF PURITAN NOMENCLATURE*)

From-above: come down.

Free-gift: breathe through the fever.

More-fruit: make sweet what's given.

Faint-not: *I will take the dark part of your heart into my heart.*

Praise-god Barebone: a pyre of sleeves for my lady's grace.

If-Christ-had-not-died-for-thee-thou-hadst-been-damned
   Barebone: live again.

Fear-god Barebone: *you run like a herd of luminous deer.*

Learn-wisdom and Hate-evil: quiverful of children,
   alchemists hale to prison.

Tribulation Wholesome, Zeal-of-the-land Busy: deliver us.

Safe-on-Highe, Muche-merceye, Increased, Sin-denie,
   Lambkin: gentle always gentle.

Sorry-for-sin Copuard: No-merit Vynall: Continent
   Walker:
   you are covered in silt and wearing the antlers again.

Preserved Fish: the only childe left in the sea.

Job-rakt-out-of-the-asshes: alive one day, a little pigeon-
   hole among the sheep.

These names went to Virginia, and they are not forgotten.

Joy-in-sorrow: who saw visions.

The bastard Helpless Henly: buried in skillful rain.

Peregrine, be useful: one day this pain will be patient with
   you.

(CITY, THERE'S A PRAYER FOR YOU)

City, there's a prayer for you.
I'm just not the one to pray it.
I gave up God years ago,
before all our deaths,
when my father put down
a salt lick at the edge of the woods,
and deer gathered there, resigned,
strange ocean at their feet,
and took what they could.
We stood at the window,
eating potato chips, my sister
just a baby, her head soft
and alive, mouthing the crib wall.
I was just a boy, and knew
the deer had spirits looking
out for them, spirits of former deer.
I would find their beds rounded
among the long grasses,
or in the needles of the tall pines,
a pattern unlike any other grafted
into the land. Down the field,
over the marsh, the outboards chugged
past the oyster beds, a night barge late
through the morning scattered
sparrows from the fish-house eaves.
I walked into that summer alone,
no deer pulled me,

no ghost led me to the salt,
light unborrowed, dead grass,
deep in the briared loam,
my tongue on loan from some
other country, copperheads
in the last sun, seed ticks
under the nettles like moonlight.
Let me be one of them.

DEPARTMENT OF ACOUSTIC APPLIANCES

I listen to July on the bricks, the weeds growing tall
below the heat. At the bottom of the hill,
three metal bands in the old box factory
churn out their simultaneous reliquaries,
sped-up prayers to no one in particular.
It is always postwar here.
Some days I want to give it all back,
this house, the neighborhood, the city,
to the silt and the wolves, the long flocks
of the sea folded and alluvial inside the clay.
But that's not my decision. Instead, I turn
the porch light on for the spider, the bulb
brings gnats and soon the whole web is alive
and shining, as if evening could only begin
with these small deaths. Instead, I buy outdoor
furniture, citronella, gas for the mower, which is
the opposite of giving it back. I throw seed
to the pigeons because the whip-poor-wills of my youth
are now pigeons, no more *chuck-will's-widow*
through the low pines, signaling down the meadow
and the years, a living radio mouthing news to the wind,
quarried from the architecture of some child's song
in an old dead time. It isn't enough, but I'll take
what I can get. Look, there I am, a man
bent at fixing himself somewhere, in the space
between our being and the earth that is.

TINTYPE

I've found my name

        in two cemeteries.

How do you measure it?

        All those lives out there.

TWO

TINTYPE

I wish I was a shepherd

        telling you this.

It would mean more, somehow,

        coming from a guy like that,

like me,

        if I was a shepherd

        and you were you.

THE NIGHT NAMES EACH BUILDING

It's like the wind without wind,
more skin than skin.
When the shroud is removed,
sometimes a forest replaces the house.
Mostly it's houses, though,
sober with winter,
suspended in river water,
sun clinging the shore,
a great rush of a life calling tender
from the past, drawn and quartered,
sent tired through the locks.
The old tracks by the river flood
and unflood, bringing up
the cobblestones and the rot
of hundred-year-fish. Herons
mean nothing to me anymore,
another reminder that seeing
gives away the gift.
I am in the world,
the river recognizes this,
but I don't believe in the river.
No shroud of snow, no thickets.

TINTYPE

There is a silo I know,

        roofless, outside the city.

The farm done over, days

      effaced. It is the nothing

that shapes the trees

        to bring the land closer.

Sweet dirt

     in the silo's heart,

a sapling colics through.

        Sweet animal
in the larger darkness,

you would not believe

      what watches.

DEPARTMENT OF (AERIAL) PHOTOGRAPHY

The first memento mori was the land, clots of sea sewn from the horizon, the amoeba with a microscope and a shovel finding its way through the burned district. It's enough of a reminder to see it from up here. In the fields there is the death clock shaped from sweet potato mounds and the face is looking not toward us, but inward, deep in the frost of 10,000 feet.

•

If every photograph is a catastrophe that has already oc-curred, as Barthes says, and every camera is a clock for seeing, I measure my life through the intervals of land-scape: what lasts, what still moves, disintegration loop of two foxes at dawn, always two foxes, always the oak, the government plane documents the land and through this we remain.

Borges, say it louder this time: *We forget that we are all dead men conversing with dead men.* Persimmons on the dirt road, fire ants expand and rise through the hurt they bring. Part of me disappeared in the blackberry. If I have a spirit, it will walk the vines, blood beads along its wrist.

•

To make a dead map mimic a living one, there must be some small mortality. Oblivion must be appeased. A boy choosing a field so the sky can see him. A sky choosing a boy so the field can sleep.

I write this as souvenir, bottling the landscape's inability to reconcile, to endure our constant need to translate what is no longer. I am the witness in animal clothes, frustrated by the failure of the afterlife, grotesque at the tobacco field's edge. There is no century to pull apart. The sweet-gum tree drops its little children into my father's truck bed, giving up all allegiance to the coming frost.

•

My ancestors, my dead men, my dead dog's grave, I hear you through the radio static, the Christian station's joyous AM lilt. Between the towers night wades the marshes, mortars the cattails, hammers into the red swell of sand.

This land is brutal in my memory; I do not forgive the velvet ants crackling my heels like radio dials. I do not forgive time's disguise: roadkill of my youth on Sloop Point Road to which we have been condemned. I do not forgive the sour grass for taking my tongue, the yellow jackets against my ears with venom. I do not forgive the blister of years' unlit rooms, Rudy Nixon drowning at 17, his mother on the floor of the church writhing toward his casket, and all the white kids terrified of their own muddled grief. Christopher Smart said *For the method of curing an ague by terror is exaction.* And I do not forgive him.

•

A wreath of shotgun shells for the deer beds, not as warning but as forgiveness for their childhoods. It disappeared into history.

I feel that the photograph creates my body, then bears it away. It is no longer mine—the rooms where we slept and bled now contain other bodies that are not ours. This is how ruin begins.

•

I pull from my mouth a clotted vine in the house that blood made. The trees are one tree and they make a human sound. On the radio, foxes broadcast lists of grievances too quickly for the translator: [*very poor recording until sixteen seconds*] ??? Mice. The ??? . ??? . ??? . ??? in the field. ??? in the right field. ??? . [We offer this ??? here (?)]. [??? rabbit not frog (?)]. We ??? . Algae tree ??? . We don't have to ??? they don't bother us. We guess they didn't bother us. Tell us. What night ??? Our father ??? one portion of ??? . [*they deliver a prayer*]

Aurelius: *Consider also what the vital spirit is: a current of air, not even continuously the same, but every hour being expelled and sucked in again.*

•

A penny nail in a foot travels slow to the lung. Pray then for the toes that bless this glorious and noble dirt.

Foxtail and clover: we unspeak each other. Fog linens down the morning, indicates change, the almanac says, and maybe it's right, negating the land and the air and the swamp fires in the north. Fog is obvious, palpable, there is a swelling, a murmur in the docks, and from the tree line it comes, a body on a cooling board pushed by a small hand of wind.

•

Faulkner, I do not know how to hold the dead. Are there ways? . . . *I give you the mausoleum of all hope and desire. . . . I give it to you not that you may remember time, but that you might forget it now and then for a moment and not spend all of your breath trying to conquer it.*

Once, the woods after twilight left us haloed in devout ruin.

•

There is something my mother told me. How the sea is simply light in an empty room and what came before the sea is a photograph of an open window in the room next to it, crease of sand, a lamp turned on. There is something Walter Benjamin told me. *To articulate the past historically does not mean to recognize it "the way it really was." It means to seize hold of a memory as it flashes up at a moment of danger.*

I did not see God in the trees. What leaves there were
pulled from the light a burdensome figure, Vaseline jar
stored in the dead pine. A biscuit in each hand for the
pigs flooding the field, all slop-mouthed and breeching.

•

The work of memory collapses time, Benjamin says. But this
isn't time I'm talking about. It's translating water, the little
fish I called aspirin-eye silver and white and alive in the
creek. Landscape was nothing more than a burden, a poor
name for the earth that was already mine.

TINTYPE

Two dresses hang

       in a backyard garden.

   Neither speaks.

THREE

For the names and number of animals
are as the name and number of the stars.

CHRISTOPHER SMART

FOR THE ANIMAL

For the animal gives us a way to reason with God.

For the animal goes from the house to the field in phases.

For the animal was a communication and is now a shroud.

For the animal takes depths to its shins and cuts the terror.

For the animal is a language of adversary.

For the animal meets another animal with duty/living
   light/seven folds against the dunes.

For the animal awakened, unnatural, failed to love.

For the animal by candlelight washes electric through the
   storm.

For the animal is ghost, monster and truce.

For the animal bends into the creek in error, locks the
   briar, narrow crown of months tumble apart in the
   formaldehyde.

For the animal in snow chooses what to fear.

For the animal pulls glass from her sleeping foot, golden as
fog.

For the animal volunteers its illegible years to live inside
the river.

For the animal manufactures the day.

For the animal there are flowers of purpose in death.

For the animal is not ancient.

For the animal is not accident.

For the animal chooses what pain to protect.

For the animal's labor calls above the drought-lake.

For the animal lives down the hall from the drink machine.

For the animal in drink-machine light chooses the Diet
    Pepsi.

For the animal faxes flood insurance to the cattail grove.

For the animal shops for headstones online and gets a good
    deal.

For the animal wears a human face inside the silo.

For the animal watches humans circle the farmhouse well.

For the animal pulls from the taxidermy an arsenic shawl.

For the animal drapes the morning with an arsenic shawl.

For the animal embezzling funds—there is no escape.

For the animal refuses a glass of water from the sheriff's
    wife.

For the animal loves the sheriff.

For the animal creates itself on the asphalt trail.

For the animal creates itself in the truck-lot ditch.

For the animal creates itself by the factory's break room.

For the animal creates itself through the stomach of its child.

For the animal creates itself before the human birth.

For the animal creates itself covered in Saran Wrap.

For the animal creates itself through mold and guile.

For the animal invented Old Norse to abate the coming
    winter.

For the animal's narrative shows in tidal pools.

For the animal floods the field with milk shapes.

For the animal regrets what makes looking possible.

For the animal is destined to petition the dried blood of
day.

For the animal is adored and collects skins of the animal.

For the animal is obsessed and kills time with the animal.

For the animal eradicates the eternal.

For the animal hums at the blossom.

For the animal is unpleasant in the marsh and the salt that
clings.

For the animal binds us to our boyhood sickness.

For the animal signals the machine with its one good eye.

For the animal holds the nail gun against the rotted foot.

For the animal in the garden of brokenness heals.

For the animal is recognized as the animal, a force like
water, an artificial thing.

For the animal is whiteness on the horizon, reduced.

For the animal is observable in the wake of ships.

For the animal sets its bed under glass as though it had
been living.

For the animal corked in rosin stops the progress of evil.

For the animal arranges its skin as if still awake.

For the animal encounters no barrier in its invisibility.

For the animal speaks through its knife by trophy and
landscape.

For the animal as souvenir gives voice to grief, to the sun
that lights it.

For the animal in the abandoned house is worthy in its
  petition to endure.
For the animal violates the blood it is given near the yards
  and highways.
For the animal presses its face against the glass of summer.
For the animal tears away the slaughter.
For the animal in the GEICO commercial glows blue with
  heat.
For the animal at the keyboard cherishes what is no longer.
For the animal fragments itself on the electric fence.
For the animal is the absence of the marvelous child.
For the animal is the marvelous child at the quarry's edge.
For the animal is the original violence.

For the animal swims the quarry in child clothes.

For the animal hides the seams to keep the suit authentic.

For the animal is witness to the disaster.

For the animal tells a story to itself about itself.

For the animal is someone else's souvenir.

For the animal's usefulness is exhausted.

For the animal is frustrated by the failure of the Dallas
Cowboys.

For the animal is frustrated by the failure of the afterlife.

For the animal in the mirror translates the cicada husk.

For the animal is grotesque at the tobacco field's edge.

For the animal and human overlap where silt meets iris
stiffened to lung.
For the animal takes silence from the milk.
For the animal takes milk from the poor.
For the animal is grub-strung—its hunger lifts the rotted log.
For the animal's mouth *will be the mouth of those griefs that
have no mouth.*
For the animal's honeyed eye collides with the dawn.
For the animal is belly-swell, is flood-face, is brackish-
tooth, is there.
For the animal *is docile and can learn certain things.*
For the animal surveys the atmosphere from a ladder of
withering blood.
For the animal in black needlerush pulls apart the century.

For the animal was a girl once and was afraid.

For the animal was a dead man in the sweet-gum tree.

For the animal's affliction is unreliable and coats the grass like arms, like wind.

For the animal removes its wig to show its useful home.

For the animal transmits its grievances on the black sound of lice.

For the animal remembers evil and sends out fires that are very like stars.

For the animal in 1900 taps on the window to test its muscle against life.

For the animal is a godless brother sleeping in your garage.

For the animal rubs its money cup on the amputee's wheelchair.

For the animal's room ails, hymn-to-hymn, graffiti on the bridge-sway, a tourniquet.

For the animal hires drug dogs to lick the blood from its
  eyes.
For the animal swells and flattens.
For the animal *can give to a mute fish the notes of a nightingale.*
For the animal on brackish water troubles through the
  plastic tide.
For the animal confesses its pink lungs to the frost.
For the animal hollows a flute for the wind.
For the animal was here, and will come again.
For the animal in cul-de-sac dark sentinels the birch.
For the animal in bed eating chips doesn't remember you at
  all.
For the animal dies for you in several ways.

For the animal lives inside another animal and there is
nothing we can do.
For the animal is not dead—it lives in us by poverty and
sun.
For the animal envies the tall grass on the interstate
median—it lives for no one.
For the animal comes back as old hatred, winter moonlight
on the dunes.
For the animal is brutal in its memory—its secret body
rages under the field.
For the animal is conditional—it is not our silence to
know.
For the animal has no name for "animal"—what a strange
thing to say.
For the animal goes on to find the wilderness, to visit the
place where names burst like clouds.
For the animal is far away, moving among the statues.
For the animal did not notice the stillness until the pines
went black.

For the animal is a loneliness, and like all lonelinesses, rests
in the Museum of Rope.

For the animal is surprised to be alive.

For the animal replaces abundance with Klonopin.

For the animal flickers in the alley among the red cans.

For the animal empties the trees with buckshot.

For the animal forms a song on its teeth and it sounds like
sleep.

For the animal makes a wreath from 12-gauge cartridges.

For the animal in your childhood makes the wrong
irredeemable.

For the animal does not forgive the childhoods.

For the animal is the absence of the stubborn world.

For the animal *it is not grief that works: grief keeps watch.*

For the animal drags its wing along the chain-link fence.

For the animal does not belong to death—it assumes
   suffering is natural.

For the animal tries to understand the sound of whiteness
   over the city.

For the animal buries stolen bread under the couch
   cushion.

For the animal is transparent against the floodwall ruin.

For the animal's citizenship is revoked, solemnly and with
   great sincerity.

For the animal crosses the county line out by the old
   lumberyard and does not look back at the falling snow.

For the animal creeks the trap, slantwise, locked by copse,
   by hollow.

For the animal wears the laughing gas suit.

For the animal is sleepy-time, is bye-bye, is numb-knees, is
  jewel-weed, is sorry.
For the animal *can take the face out of the lake but not the lake
  out of the face.*
For the animal leads the doe through the blizzard,
  gunnysack and all.
For the animal unsettles the hatchlings from lavender's ash
  trap.
For the animal mimeographs *pin bones & ice fish & pine-leaf
  . . . wind . . . & star.*
For the animal's apparatus measures light pollution, the
  sound of whiteness over the city.
For the animal tunnels lichen from the lantern's sad rain.
For the animal's evening thaws enough to break the
  interstate, one new widow in fever.
For the animal takes field notes in the vacant house—there
  is a coastline nearby, a heron tendon-soft, a window
  closes on the wind's marrowed hand.
For the animal mourns the invention of suburbs, lamblike
  in the stalls, crickets crushed between bales.

For the animal is uninspired, yawns over the doe-bed in
   honey-faced light.
For the animal's fish-scrawl cuffs the snow at sea.
For the animal is maybe a music ailing past dawn into the
   smallest white source.
For the animal, wounded, runs the tree line mathematics.
For the animal is *a white sheet drawn behind the objects.*
For the animal wrings out its T-shirt, the river in fog, the
   bricks pleat in a drywall pile, worm-sick, appeased.
For the animal mosquitoes the veil, reblooms the air, sorts
   through the hailstones for the right twilight.
For the animal comforts no moon, breathes the
   woodsmoke meadow.
For the animal bears what you cannot.
For the animal thought you would never ask.

DEPARTMENT OF TAXIDERMY

The land is an incarnation
Like a hand on a hand on an arm asking do you know me?
—FANNY HOWE

Sometimes I try to see the city as a taxidermist would: the wind as armature announces the skin, pigeons stain the air, graph and vein in the bread factory's cloak. Underneath it all the landscape, orphan tissue, pelt trussed with rebar and lung, arsenic bodies where every parking lot used to be a house, every foundation a grove of elm. Here, the buried cobblestones are coughing through the asphalt. Here, the buried slaves are coughing up the graves that built them.

To make a dead hill mimic a living one there must be some minor immortality. One thousand glass eyes down the sleeves of the Confederate re-enactors guarding the Lee monument, an implied movement of wing, of tail, but *even movement is a form of property,* the anarchist down the street says. Herons mounted on the island across from the old hydro plant could be mistaken as malfunction. Ownership congealed with nonbeing. I own yet I am nothing.

This neighborhood could still kill me if it wanted to. The dealer with the blue eyes of a foal. The old woman with the Army pack and the hunting knife running for the bus. She said hello to me yesterday and it hurt to know her like this. My neighbor found a human hip bone in his crawl space. Not mine, but might as well be. The grackles mouthed chicken bones in the street and brought them to my yard to invent a finer bird, coaxed from the gristle, the hydrangea.

There must be a better way to keep the animals with us. Aren't ghosts enough? The fur-rimmed shawl of night is a warmth, not a darkness. When there is another darkness, I'll admit it. What makes you think I'm enjoying this? I say *arsenic* but I mean *memory*, or *governance*, some kind of control over the night. I mean *childhood*.

Sometimes it gets lonely here. There is rain, and there isn't. The river tells us nothing, absolutely nothing. It floods, it dries. It does what rivers do. I want more from it, it's got to know more, smuggled under the floorboards. *An animal bed in a holy room.* All those years underneath it. There is no better life. There is this. The dogs bark, but not for us.

FOUR

Gabriel, today commonly—if incorrectly—known as Gabriel Prosser, was a literate enslaved blacksmith who planned a large slave rebellion in the Richmond area in the summer of 1800. Information regarding the revolt was leaked prior to its execution, and he and twenty-five followers were taken captive and hanged in punishment.

———————

Memory lives in the breath we breathe, in the air we make together.

JAKE ADAM YORK

MEMORIAL DEPARTMENT

North up 24th Street a fire truck laments
past my porch to the projects where someone
is rising through the living body of Sunday afternoon
in flames. I felt the siren's incompletion follow me
inside, holding to its failure, the air easily harmed,
scaffolds of the tulip tree botched with mites
and it doesn't seem to want to not rain.
I need to feel that I'm better than this, the tree,
the siren, all of it, to devise a way to mend a life,
maybe not even mine. The stray dogs choking down
chicken bones in the market's trash don't even
consider me, rope leashes dauntless in dust,
no names, former lives they recall only in passing scents:
work glove, Lysol, chain link, hot dog.
The bread factory is beyond help, is now condos,
and the water tower on its roof pumped dry,
repainted, hollowed out, used to resurrect
the archaic, the idea of water not water itself.
There is no end, no destination.
Should I feel nostalgia or just defeat
about a bread crumb poultice
on the stray German shepherd's neck, the work
of an old hand that has not forgotten how to mend?
Gabriel in the gallows, do not misunderstand.
This is meant to signify ache, someone other than me.
When I write *under the hospital cobbles,* two swallows
pull a crow down. *Ghost rope taut* means the horizon

looms the rain, neighborhoods dim, the parking lot
empties and medical students in their scrubs drive past
the boarded-up sandwich shop and over your grave.
Come and start a new country. I swear there is hope
in vacancy, in Mini Coopers and stethoscopes, dialysis,
ibuprofen, warehouse rats. When I write *orphan,*
another fire truck rolls by, numerous engines catch
and ignite, catch and ignite, the meaning of a history
is its animal, its curse. *Architecture* rejects, descends,
the crabgrass cruel between sidewalk bricks.
I cannot begin to tell you how cities are founded.
There was never one place I belonged. I came from an egg,
from under the raspberry bush where to dream of blood
meant your children will perish from the face of the earth.
I do not think you will remember me.
Gabriel in the gallows, decay doesn't begin, it was here
the whole time. *Ruin* can mean anything you want it to mean.
It could even be a method of devotion.
Look at the highway, so close to your grave.
The trucks roaring by make a routine wind
in the guardrail's rigging and you are not that wind.
My words are less than the touch of its rising.
It's getting late. I've walked down here
to disown my past, and now I can't make out
the telephone poles from the trees, each one
buzzing the black droplets of night from wire
to branch, transformer to leaf, as if night
was engineered, a system for us to console,
then grieve. Regret comes to me like this,

standing here in your parking lot next to
the forgotten sandwich shop. Last year
a storm took down the old wooden sign,
Sandwiches, black-on-white gravestone
of no reverence, no memory, the one
I coveted for its charm, weathered
from all the working-class mouths repeating
through the years, *sandwiches, sandwiches.*
There shall be no famine, there shall be no fear.
What a lovely, simple word.
When I write it to you, all the world goes out.

LETTER TO GABRIEL WRITTEN IN THE
MARGINS OF *MURDER BALLADS*

Here is a story in the worst way. I have no business being
*   anywhere in it.*
It comes between me and the life I have coming.
    —GARY LUTZ

Blood of my abyss, illegible voice, was the morning kind?

The cold dawns here, steaming through.

I imagine you in a field
across the river, floodplain attic,
lichen brailed thin on the pump-house door.

You are dead in the gallows and not dead,
the rope cannot claim you.

It is another century.

Things are not better or worse.

You came without a horse
and left us human hair in the tulip tree,
strange among the blossoms.

For years we weren't terrified,
we carried around your death, its severity.

The terror lasts, your grave a wide field now,
but I never thought of it as something separate.

Jake gone six months, then seven.
I move through summer, verb for breath, accrue.

Heat understands, folds into the dashboards.

A woman is living in her Oldsmobile on Leigh Street.
For weeks she unfolds the traffic,
the shade of an elm pours, devalues,
all present tense and bending close,
house to house. There is no explaining
the ghost of a face, then a face.

What can I give that won't be taken,
assembled into guilt? The feral cat
under the shed archives the rats, then squirrels.

Gone isn't the word I'm looking for.

There's no other way to say it:
I was built by slaves,
carved skin white-pined
like sand and tobacco
and the Poteat name
that pulls me from you.

Say the words
the fields would speak.

The bloodline stops
here.

All the sleeping Poteats.
All their skin, impossible to see.
All their land and gauzed light.
All the asphalt and rain between us.
All the kerosene on the carpet,
kudzu weaving doors shut.
All great-great-grandfathers gutting
pigs. All great-grandmothers
throwing sand on the blood.
All industry siphoned.
All selves creek-banked, collapsed.
All plantations a coffin, a little vandalism.
The whole family, haunted.

I've played the slave narratives
in abandoned places—
among the candles
and cinder blocks.

Silo, dirt, house
where the vultures live.

All to bring you back.

There's a shopping mall
where your anvil stood.

I bought socks, a button-down shirt,
and sat in the parking lot listening
to the corroded wax cylinders—
disintegrating dialects
becoming a column of air
anyone can pass through.

I never deserved to hear them.

[*opening incomprehensible, very poor recording until one minute
    sixteen seconds*]

[*equipment set-up noise and pause*]

[*steam engine toots in background*]

[*disc skips*]

[*a cat meows*]

[(?)]

[*loud gurgling sound*]

[*Mrs. Annie Williams sings*]

[*loud distortion*]

[*she delivers a prayer*]

[*microphone noise before Uncle Billy sings*]

[*he attempts to sing*]

[*the women seem to hold a discussion among themselves*]

[*concludes song*]

[*Mrs. Williams sings*]

[*remainder of recording extremely poor*]

God is ??? of God my ???

[*recording ends*]

Woo-Woo turned a trick in the Rent-a-Toilet
last night. I watched her pull the man in,
septic dark pocked with paper towels,
clefts of rain.

The world was one place, then overnight,
it became someplace else.

In other words, this is always going to be
about mine, not yours.

I am teaching myself to see the street
as sleep is seen:

Woo-Woo with a toothache, jaw looped
with panty hose. Even mentioning her
is a gentrification.

I make it sound like I know an answer.

She is not you and we honor this emptiness.

When the highway came, the houses
didn't know enough to be afraid.
Leeway and ease, night comes
through the gutters loose as fever.

I don't believe there is an answer,
honeysuckle blooming the creek gut.

There are tunnels leading up from the river,
dug before the war. Torch ends
grating in their cups, history averting
into the cellars of abolitionists.

This is not what I mean to say to you.

Jake gone eight months,
even the honeysuckle estranges,
pleats the afternoon.

Everything is unfinished, momentary.
It's not anyone's fault, I know.

We're all strangers to the middle of the noise.

On *Live at Birdland,* Coltrane's "Alabama" drops
the snare by the church parking lot at 2:42.

That's where the ghosts are,
waiting with the floor tom,
a tousled mess of glyph and syllable.

Child of gravity, stranger to the ground.
Come down and help me rise.

The jessamine cut back, the wisteria ordered
and blunt from the rails. We have to be humble
or we're taken down.

How many examples do you need?
Soft as milk-shaped light in the halfway house
where the sex offenders live.

An owl in another country invented night.

You must remember
this is not about history.

It's about finding where life enters our deaths.

I do not bring you to the river beneath the river
because time ruins, a heresy.

The river erases itself when we need it most,
dawn inside dawn, tar in the throat of the oak,
a hermit thrush strange and metallic over
Jefferson Park repeats the vowels its body carves.
A fine ash of song too far south.

A house is taken from the landscape
and the wind blows stronger
through that space.
The body can't signify
that kind of vacancy.

Always one of everything here . . . one bee in the clover,
one dove on the power line, one mockingbird
diving into the jessamine to guard its one chick
that will be dead by Sunday.

I can see the layers of need
where I couldn't before: first a sea,
an orchard, a corral, a parking lot.

There is nothing left of the sea here
but its sound, street cleaner flushing
the day out, brushes like wings under
their machinery, star's blood through
the pipes under the street, watershed
of the river and farther out, the bay.

Jake, gone almost a year.
Woo-Woo, gone. Feral cat, gone.

Harry's down the street fixing
his station wagon in the cold.
He said the cops used
my house in the '80s to watch
the dealers on the corner.

The whole block abandoned back then.

Sniper in the bay window, dead man
on the bricks. 19 arrested.

The black stain on the bedroom floor
refutes the belt sander, shifts
from history to history,
outliving us, passing deeper.

Stanley's drunk again, his walk
more song than speech.
He asked me once if I was rich.

The porch fell off Scott's house
and made the news. Someone's
burning wood this evening,
the Masonic Lodge quiet.

I lean from the window
to feel it slip past me.
All of it.

There is only one year,
and it repeats itself forever.

Forfeit the dead grass,
the rim of dandelion
and mortgage. Forfeit
the factory where the marrow
is pulled. Forfeit taxonomy,
the legalese of the law office
windows at sunset, so many
*heretofore*s and *to wit*s. Forfeit foreclosure,
the vacant lots, stairs leading to white
grass and sunlight. Where houses
were sewn together, now gone.
Foundations, the absence
of ruin is just as quiet, nonbeing
where was being, remains.

The old theater on 25th Street,
sunk in ivy, the roof long gone
or the roof is the sky . . . either way
there's nothing there, saplings crowd
the orchestra pit, mud wasps
in the projection booth, flicker of
pornography and sun hollowing the years.

I have never been hungry.

You invented hunger and handed it to the owl,
200-year-old crime-scene tape slung from the bridges.

What should the new map look like?

Help me, moonlight.

Bring the granary to the sky,
burnt yellow called down.

The night that took you
will take us too.

NOTES

DRUG DEPARTMENT

I'm looking for a story to light my way out.

SUSANN COKAL

LIGHTING DEPARTMENT

What do you want, brick?

LOUIS KAHN

The centuries will float to me . . . out of the darkness.

BORIS PASTERNAK

DEPARTMENT OF HYMNALS

The year before I die
I shall send out four hymns to track down God.

TOMAS TRANSTRÖMER

VETERINARY DEPARTMENT

The dead do not know who I am.

ADAM CLAY

DEATH OF THE DEATH OF YOUTH

I see the summer children in their mothers.

DYLAN THOMAS

The noise of time is not sad.

ROLAND BARTHES

. . . Who kills my history?

DYLAN THOMAS

I am the man your father was . . .

DYLAN THOMAS

We are the sons of flint and pitch.

DYLAN THOMAS

THE NIGHT NAMES EACH BUILDING

Sometimes a forest replaces the house.

COLE SWENSEN

No shroud of snow, no thickets.

ANN MARSHALL

DEPARTMENT OF NAMES

I will take the dark part of your heart into my heart.

PERFUME GENIUS

. . . you run like a herd of luminous deer.

RAINER MARIA RILKE

ALL NAMES TAKEN FROM *Curiosities of Puritan Nomenclature,* 1888.

FOR THE ANIMAL

. . . will be the mouth of those griefs that have no mouth.

AIMÉ CÉSAIRE

. . . *is docile and can learn certain things.*

CHRISTOPHER SMART

. . . *can give to a mute fish the notes of a nightingale.*

CHRISTOPHER SMART

. . . *it is not grief that works: grief keeps watch.*

MAURICE BLANCHOT

. . . *can take the face out of the lake but not the lake out of the face.*

JULIA COHEN

. . . *pin bones & ice fish & pine-leaf . . . wind . . . & star.*

ANN MARSHALL

. . . *a white sheet drawn behind the objects.*

JOHN CONSTABLE

DEPARTMENT OF TAXIDERMY

An animal bed in a holy room.

DYLAN THOMAS

LETTER TO GABRIEL WRITTEN IN THE MARGINS OF *MURDER BALLADS*

It is another century.
Things are not better or worse.

NORMAN DUBIE

The world was one place, then overnight,
it became someplace else.

GARY LUTZ

In other words, this is always going to be
about mine, not yours.

GARY LUTZ

What should the new map look like?

FROM THE FILM *General Orders No. 9*, ROBERT PERSONS,

2009

ACKNOWLEDGMENTS

Special thanks to these institutions/people for giving me time/ money/support in which to write: The College of William & Mary Donaldson Writer in Residence Program—Henry Hart, Nancy Schoenberger, and all of my amazing students; Virginia Commonwealth University; Carole Weinstein and the Virginia Center for Creative Arts; Norton Island/Eastern Frontier Educational Foundation; The Martin Agency—especially Nancy Foltz, Jean Hughes, and Mike Hughes—for giving me an office on the seventeenth floor with a view that I don't deserve in which many of these poems were conceived (not on company time, of course); Ward Tefft, Andrew Blossom, and Chop Suey Books.

Extra special thanks to: National Poetry Series/Lannan Foundation; Campbell McGrath; Stephanie Stio; Sydney Pierce and HarperCollins; Ander Monson and Diagram/New Michigan Press.

Without these people, this book would be filled with even more regret than it already is: Allison Titus, Jake Adam York, Gabe Lovejoy, Kira Poteat, Roberto Ventura, Ann Marshall, Ethan Bullard, Kelly Kerney, Heather Treseler, and the neighborhood of Church Hill, Richmond, Virginia.

ABOUT THE AUTHOR

JOSHUA POTEAT is the author of three books, *The Regret Histories, Illustrating the Machine That Makes the World,* and *Ornithologies,* as well as three chapbooks: *The Scenery of Farewell (and Hello Again), For the Animal,* and *Meditations.* His poems have appeared in *Virginia Quarterly Review, The Southern Review, Ninth Letter, Blackbird, Gulf Coast, Typo, Diode, Handsome,* and many others. He has also won numerous awards and fellowships from the Poetry Society of America, Virginia Commission for the Arts, Vermont Studio Center, The Millay Colony, The College of William & Mary, *American Literary Review, Bellingham Review, Columbia: A Journal of Literature & Art, Hunger Mountain, Marlboro Review, Nebraska Review,* and others. Poteat lives in Richmond, Virginia.